KU-441-314

Wonderful weekly English practice from CGP!

This book is packed with brilliant Workouts to help Year 1 pupils practise their English skills in 10-Minute chunks every week.

Each Workout covers a mixture of topics — all carefully matched to the Year 1 English curriculum. Use them for starter activities, recaps, homework tasks... or any way that suits you!

We've also included a progress chart and full answers, so it's easy to track how pupils are getting on. It's all worked out beautifully...

Published by CGP

ISBN: 978 1 78908 313 2

Editors: Hannah Roscoe and Matt Topping

With thanks to Gabrielle Richardson and Lucy Towle for the proofreading.

With thanks to Jan Greenway for the copyright research.

Images throughout the book from www.edu-clips.com

Printed by Elanders Ltd, Newcastle upon Tyne.

Based on the classic CGP style created by Richard Parsons.

Text, design, layout and original illustrations
© Coordination Group Publications Ltd. (CGP) 2019
All rights reserved.

How to Use this Book

- This book contains <u>36 workouts</u>. We've split them into <u>3 sections</u>, one for each term, with <u>12 workouts</u> each. There's roughly one workout for <u>every week</u> of the school year.

- Each workout is out of <u>10 marks</u> and should take about <u>10 minutes</u> to complete.

- Each workout tests a variety of <u>English content</u> from the government's <u>programme of study</u>, including grammar, punctuation, spelling, comprehension and writing skills.

- The workouts build on skills learnt in <u>Reception</u> and introduce new topics for <u>Year 1</u>.

- The <u>last 9</u> workouts <u>recap</u> the topics covered in <u>Year 1</u>. These workouts should be done at the <u>end</u> of Year 1.

- As the book progresses, the tests increase in <u>difficulty</u>. If pupils are struggling with the <u>terminology</u>, they can turn to the <u>glossary</u> on p.81.

- <u>Answers</u> can be found at the <u>back</u> of the book.

The <u>contents page</u> will help you identify which Year 1 <u>statutory requirement</u> is being tested in each workout. You can use these to pick the workout which best <u>suits</u> you and the needs of your class (but remember the <u>later</u> in the book, the <u>harder</u> the workout will be, so it's best to save the workouts towards the end of the book for <u>later in the year</u>).

There is a <u>tick box</u> next to each workout on the contents page. Use this to <u>record</u> which tests have been attempted. You can also use the <u>progress chart</u> to track pupils' scores.

Contents — Autumn Term

Contents — Spring Term

Contents — Summer Term

10

Warm up

1. **Cross out** the word which is **spelt wrong**.

    hee / he

    ___
    1 mark

2. **Complete** these words with '**ff**' or '**ll**'.
    Use the **pictures** to help you.

    be............   cli............   do............

    ___
    3 marks

3. **Tick** the sentence which uses **spaces** correctly.

    Jameslikesjam.   ☐

    James likes jam.   ☐

    ___
    1 mark

4. **Circle** the words which rhyme with **sail**.

rail   call

boy   tail

2 marks

5. Put these pictures in the **right order** to tell a story.
   Write either **2**, **3** or **4** in the boxes to continue the story.

☐   1   ☐   ☐

3 marks

Score: ☐

Warm up

1. Add the missing **letter** to each of the words below.
    Use the **pictures** to help you.

ra.....   bi.....   bo.....

3 marks

2. **Circle** the words that end with **nk**.

pink   duck

bank   cloak

2 marks

3. **Circle** the words which are **spelt correctly**.

leg / leag   beag / beg

2 marks

4. **Tick** the **two** sentences that **make sense**.

Ball I have a. ☐

We went to the park. ☐

They a film saw. ☐

Ellie loves her dog. ☐

2 marks

5. **Copy** the sentence below.

She made a cake.

....

....

1 mark

Score: ☐

Autumn Term: Workout 3

Warm up

1. **Cross out** the word which is **spelt wrong**.

   go   /   gow

   _____
   1 mark

2. **Complete** these words with '**ss**' or '**zz**'.
   Use the **pictures** to help you.

   ki............   dre............   fi............

   _____
   3 marks

3. **Circle** the word which rhymes with **cook**.

   hook   cot

   pole   lock

   _____
   1 mark

6

4. **Circle** the word which needs a **capital letter**.

the cat chases a mouse.

1 mark

5. Look at the **picture** below.
   Circle all the **frogs**.

4 marks

Score:

Warm up

1. **Circle** the word that ends with **tch**.

pen   bench

path   catch

_____
1 mark

2. **Cross out** the words which are **spelt wrong**.

tni   /   tin   one   /   oen

_____
2 marks

3. **Write** 'air' in the gaps to complete the words.
   Then **draw lines** to the correct **pictures**.

ch...............   p...............

_____
2 marks

8

4. **Tick** the **two** sentences that use **full stops** correctly.

Bob walks home. ☐

I am five. years old. ☐

You play. with me ☐

The bird is singing. ☐

2 marks

5. **Write** the sentence below using **spaces**.
Use the **picture** to help you.

Thereismycat.

....

....

3 marks

Score: ☐

9

Warm up

1. **Cross out** the word which is **spelt wrong**.

    wil   /   will

    _____
    1 mark

2. **Tick** the **two** words that end with **ck**.

    walk ☐   green ☐

    pack ☐   clock ☐

    _____
    2 marks

3. **Circle** the **two** words which rhyme with **light**.

    pit   right

    tilt   kite

    _____
    2 marks

4. **Circle** the **two** words that tell you
    there is **more than one** of them.

    cows   plane

    leaf   cards

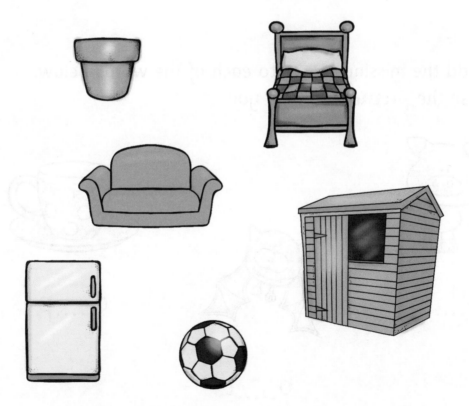

5. Look at the **pictures** below.
    Circle all the things that belong **outside**.

Score:

Warm up

1. **Tick** the sentence which uses **spaces** correctly.

   I clean the window. ☐

   I cleanthewindow. ☐

1 mark

2. Add the missing **letter** to each of the words below.
   Use the **pictures** to help you.

p.....g

b.....t

c.....p

3 marks

3. **Choose** a word from the box to **complete** the sentence.
   Use the **picture** to help you. **Write** it on the line below.

   | dove   cave   move |

   The wolf lives in a .... ____

   1 mark

4. **Circle** the words which are **spelt correctly**.

   saw / sor   corn / cawn   ____

   2 marks

5. **Write** the sentence below using **spaces**.
   Use the **picture** to help you.

   Hedigsahole.

   ....

   .... ____

   3 marks

   Score: [   ]

Autumn Term: Workout 7

Warm up

1. **Cross out** the word which is **spelt wrong**.

    are   /   arr

    _____
    1 mark

2. **Circle** the **two** words which rhyme with **shark**.

    sack   park

    curl   mark

    _____
    2 marks

3. **Draw lines** to match each word to the correct **picture**.

    apples   apple   church   churches

    _____
    2 marks

4.   **Add** '**un**' to the word below so it means the **opposite**.

..........tie

1 mark

5.   Put these pictures in the **right order** to tell a story.
     Write either **1**, **2**, **3** or **4** in the boxes to show the order.

4 marks

Score:

Warm up

1. **Circle** the word that has **ph** in it.

   rope   high

              photo   peel

   ___
   1 mark

2. Look at the letters in **bold**.
   Write **V** if it's a **vowel** and **C** if it's a **consonant**.

   j**e**t   li**p**

   ☐   ☐

   ___
   2 marks

3. **Choose** a pair of letters from the box to **complete** each word. Use the **pictures** to help you.

   | ea   oo   ew |

   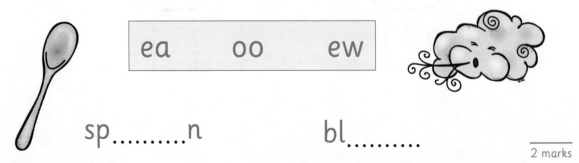

   sp.........n   bl.........

   ___
   2 marks

4. **Circle** the **two** words which need a **capital letter**.

harry

lion

i

cold

town

5. **Write** the sentence below using **spaces**.
    Use the **picture** to help you.

Janedrinkssomewater.

....

....

Score:

(10)

Warm up

1. **Cross out** the word which is **spelt wrong**.

    you   /   yoo

    _____
    1 mark

---

2. **Circle** the **two** words which have a **hard c** sound.

    smart   mood   kite

    cent   keep

    _____
    2 marks

---

3. **Tick** the sentence that uses a **capital letter** and **full stop** correctly.

    We saw a tree.   ☐

    i ride my horse.   ☐

    They read a. book   ☐

    _____
    1 mark

18

4. **Circle** the words which are **spelt correctly**.

dier / deer   hear / heer   ____
2 marks

5. Put these pictures in the **right order** to tell a story.
   Write either **1**, **2**, **3** or **4** in the boxes to show the order.

4 marks

Score:

Autumn Term: Workout 10

Warm up

1. **Circle** the word which is **spelt correctly**.

    colder   /   coldder

    _____
    1 mark

2. Add the missing **vowel** to each of the words below.
    Use the **pictures** to help you.

       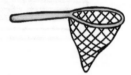

    p.....t   v.....n   n.....t

    _____
    3 marks

3. The word below is **spelt wrong**. **Rewrite** it with the
    correct spelling on the line. Use the **picture** to help you.

    coyn

    ....

    _____
    1 mark

Autumn Term: Workout 10   © CGP — not to be photocopied

20

4. **Match** each of the words below to the **correct box** on the right.

button

noses

foxes

bench

one thing

more than one thing

2 marks

5. **Write** the sentence below using a **capital letter** and a **full stop**.

she brushed her teeth

....

....

3 marks

Score:

Warm up

1. **Circle** the **correct spelling** of the day of the week.

   Sonday   /   Sunday

2. Look at the word below.
   Write **V** under the **vowels** and **C** under the **consonants**.

   s   a   l   t

   ☐   ☐   ☐   ☐

3. **Circle** the words that end with **ing**.

   buying   hides

   song   finding

4. Add '**ir**' or '**ur**' to the words below.
    Use the **pictures** to help you.

I st.......... the mixture.

My rabbit has long f...........

I like your sh..........t.

3 marks

5. Add a **letter** to the word **sock** to show that
    Abed lost **more than one** sock. Then **write**
    the full sentence on the lines.

Abed lost his sock.......

....

....

2 marks

Score:

Autumn Term: Workout 12

Warm up

1. Add the missing **vowel** to each of the words below.
    Use the **pictures** to help you.

h.....nd   m.....lk

2 marks

2. **Circle** the **pairs of consonants** in each word.

t r i p   c l o s e

2 marks

3. **Cross out** the words that are **spelt wrong**.

said   pul

me   twoday

2 marks

24

4. **Tick** the **two** sentences that use **spaces** correctly.

I sawatiger. ☐

I saw a tiger. ☐

Myauntlives there. ☐

My aunt lives there. ☐

2 marks

5. **Copy** the sentences below.

My dad likes carrots. I hate them.

....

....

....

2 marks

Score: ☐

Warm up

1. **Cross out** the words which are **spelt wrong**.

   look / luk   intoo / into   _____

   2 marks

2. **Tick** the **two** sentences that use '**and**' **correctly**.

   I like ham and cheese. ☐

   You have and a cat. ☐

   The dog is black and white. ☐

   We can and swim run. ☐

   2 marks

3. The word below is **spelt wrong**. **Rewrite** it with the
   correct spelling on the line. Use the **picture** to help you.

   wale

   ....

   1 mark

4. **Choose** a pair of letters from the box to **complete** each word. Use the **pictures** to help you.

| oa | o_e | ow |

c.....n.....   s.........p

2 marks

5. Look at the **pictures** below. Then **answer** the questions.

Amir   Fatima   Kim   Josh

Who wears a cap?   ....

Who wears glasses?   ....

Who wears a bow?   ....

3 marks

Score:

Warm up

1. Add the **missing vowel** to each of the words below.
   Use the **pictures** to help you.

sp.....t   pl.....m

_____
2 marks

2. **Match** each word to the correct number of **syllables**.

hotdog		1

tent		2

_____
2 marks

3. Put these words in the **right order** to make a sentence.
   Write either **1**, **2**, **3** or **4** in the boxes to show the order.

went   Paul   London   to

☐   ☐   ☐   ☐

_____
1 mark

4. Add 'ee' or 'ie' to the words in **bold** below.
   Use the **pictures** to help you.

My **f**.........**t** are large.

We play in the **f**.........**ld**.

It is nice to **m**.........**t** you.

5. **Write** the sentence below using **spaces**.
   Use the **picture** to help you.

Thedogchewsthebone.

....

....

Score:

10

Warm up

1. **Cross out** the words which are **spelt wrong**.

   some / sume   ful / full

   <u>   </u>
   2 marks

---

2. **Tick** the box where '**and**' should go in each sentence.

   I am ☐ tall ☐ he is short.

   I ☐ am quiet ☐ she is loud.

   <u>   </u>
   2 marks

---

3. Add the **missing letters** to each of the words below.
   Use the **pictures** to help you.

   c.......   cl.......d

   <u>   </u>
   2 marks

---

4. **Rearrange** the letters in the boxes to **complete** the words ending in '**y**'. Use the **pictures** to help you.

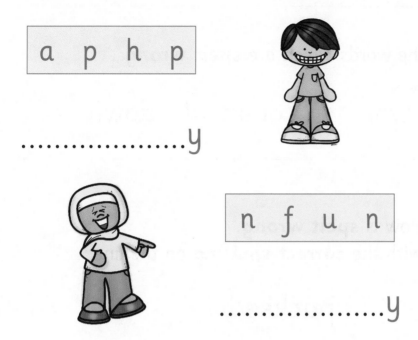

| a | p | h | p |

..................y

| n | f | u | n |

..................y

5. Add a pair of letters to the word **glass** to show that Beth washed **more than one** glass. Then **write out** the full sentence on the lines below.

Beth washed the glass..........

....

....

Score: [   ]

Warm up

1. **Cross out** the words which are **spelt wrong**.

    was / woz   doun / down

    1 mark

2. The word below is **spelt wrong**.
    Rewrite it with the **correct spelling** on the line.

    packked

    ....

    1 mark

3. **Circle** the words which have the same
    'ar' sound as the word **car**.

    bark

    share

    jar   care

    2 marks

4. **Rewrite** the words in **bold** on the lines.
   Add **letters** to show there's **more than one**.

   one **plant** ⟶ two ....

   one **dress** ⟶ two ....

   _____
   2 marks

5. Put these pictures in the **right order** to tell a story.
   Write either **1**, **2**, **3** or **4** in the boxes to show the order.

_____
4 marks

Score: [   ]

10

Warm up

1. Add the **missing letters** to each of the words below.
   Use the **pictures** to help you.

p.....s.....   f.....s.....

_____
2 marks

2. Look at the words below. They can be **joined together**
   to make **new words**. **Write** the new words on the lines.

foot + ball ⟶ ....

butter + fly ⟶ ....

_____
2 marks

3. **Circle** the **pairs of consonants** in each word.

f r o g   s h o w

_____
1 mark

4. Put a **tick** next to the sentence that ends with an **exclamation mark**. Put a **cross** next to the sentence that ends with a **question mark**.

What time is it? ☐

It is dinner time. ☐

How hungry I am! ☐

2 marks

5. **Write** the sentences below using **full stops**.

My mum eats ice cream She enjoys it

....

....

....

3 marks

Score: ☐

Warm up

1. Choose a **vowel** from the box to complete each word below.

e	i	u

    st.....p   gr.....n

    _____
    1 mark

2. Add '**ll**' or '**ss**' to the words in **bold** below.

    The snake **hi**..........**ed**.

    The **hi**......... is over there.

    _____
    2 marks

3. **Circle** the words which have the same
    short e sound as the word **pet**.

    bead

    vet   red

    need
              pea

    _____
    2 marks

4. **Circle** the **two** words which need a **capital letter**.

england   water   daniel

pizza   test

2 marks

5. Look at the **picture** below, then **read** each sentence.
If the sentence **matches** the picture, circle '**yes**'.
If it **doesn't match** the picture, circle '**no**'.

There are six animals.   yes / no

The weather is sunny.   yes / no

The farmer is happy.   yes / no

3 marks

Score:

🕙 10

Warm up

1. Add 'un' to the words below so they mean the **opposite**.

    ....do   ....roll

    1 mark

2. The words below are **spelt wrong**.
    Rewrite them with the **correct spelling** on the lines.

    asc   yor

    ....

    2 marks

3. Add a **pair of consonants** to complete the words below.
    Use the **pictures** to help you.

    The **si**.......... was full of water.

    I **thi**.......... it is correct.

    2 marks

38

4. The words below are **spelt wrong**. **Rewrite** them with the **correct spelling** on the lines. Use the **pictures** to help you.

haer

scair

....

5. **Write** the sentences below using **capital letters**.

we go to the zoo. it is lots of fun.

....

....

....

Score:

Spring Term: Workout 8

Warm up

1. Choose a **vowel** from the box to complete each word below.

a	o	i

r…..sh   h…..nt

1 mark

2. Add the letters '**oi**' or '**oy**' to each of the words below.
   Use the **pictures** to help you.

b……….l   t……….s

1 mark

3. **Circle** the words which are **spelt correctly**.

hatch / hach   ich / itch

2 marks

4. **Tick** the box where '**and**' should go in each sentence.

The room is clean ☐ tidy ☐.

They like ☐ to sing ☐ dance.

I ☐ hate peas ☐ beans.

3 marks

5. **Join** these sentences together using the word '**and**'. **Write** the new sentence on the lines.

I am short. I have big eyes.

....

....

....

3 marks

Score: ☐

Warm up

1. Add a **pair of letters** to complete the word in **bold** below. Use the **picture** to help you.

    My **glo**.........**s** are orange.

    1 mark

2. Circle the word which is **spelt wrong**.
    Rewrite it with the **correct spelling** on the line.

    hav   were

    ....

    2 marks

3. **Circle** the **correct spelling** of the words in **bold** to complete the sentences.

    I **roa / row** the boat.

    The **gowt / goat** is friendly.

    Leela wants to go **home / hoam**.

    3 marks

42

4. **Add some letters** to the **singular** words in **bold** below to make them **plural**.

Singular words tell you that there's <u>only one</u> of something. Plural words tell you that there's <u>more than one</u>.

one **bull** $\longrightarrow$ two ....

one **torch** $\longrightarrow$ two ....

2 marks

5. Put these pictures in the **right order** to tell a story. Write either **1**, **2**, **3** or **4** in the boxes to show the order.

2 marks

Score:

43

Spring Term: Workout 10

10

Warm up

1. Add the missing **letters** to each of the words below.
    Use the **pictures** to help you.

.....a.....l   b.........h

1 mark

2. **Match** each word to the correct number of **syllables**.

garden		2

radio		3

2 marks

3. Look at the sentence below. Write '**X**' in the boxes
    under the **capital letter** and **full stop** that are **wrong**.

The pig **D**igs in**.** the mud**.**

2 marks

4. **Rearrange** the letters in the boxes to make two words with the 'ai' sound. The **first letter** of each word is in **bold**.

| y | **p** | a | l |

| **g** | e | a | m |

....

5. **Join** these sentences together using the word '**and**'. **Write** the new sentence on the lines.

She bakes bread.   She makes cakes.

....

....

....

Score:

10

Warm up

1. Circle the word which is **spelt wrong**.
   Rewrite it with the **correct spelling** on the line.

   his   shee

   ....

   <u>2 marks</u>

2. Join the words and endings together to make
   new words. **Write** the new words on the lines.

   jump + ed ⟶ ....

   wish + ed ⟶ ....

   <u>2 marks</u>

3. The word below is **spelt wrong**. **Rewrite** it with the
   correct spelling on the line. Use the **picture** to help you.

   mowse

   ....

   <u>1 mark</u>

4. Add a **pair of consonants** to complete the words
    in **bold** below. Use the **pictures** to help you.

Give me a glue **sti**...........

She **li**.........**s** her ice lolly.

5. **Write** the sentences below using
    a **question mark** and a **full stop**.

How are you I am very well

....

....

....

Score:

Spring Term: Workout 12

Warm up

1. Add the missing **letters** to each of the words below.
    Use the **pictures** to help you.

     .....t.....r

     f.....a.....

    ___
    1 mark

2. Look at the sentence below.
    Circle the **two** words which need a **capital letter**.

    On monday, hannah came for tea.

    ___
    2 marks

3. **Rearrange** the letters in the boxes to make two words with
    the long 'i' sound. The **first letter** of each word is in **bold**.

e	k	**b**	i

h	t	i	g	**l**

    ....

    ___
    2 marks

48

4. Add 's' or 'es' to the words below to complete the sentences.

He throw......... the ball.

She catch......... it.

5. Look at the **picture** below. **Circle** the correct word to complete each sentence.

There is a treasure **chest / ship**.

The diver is holding a **rock / shell**.

There are four **fish / rocks**.

Score:

Warm up

1. The word below is **spelt wrong**.
    Rewrite it with the **correct spelling** on the line.

    jusst

    ....

    1 mark

2. **Finish** each sentence with a **question mark**.

    How old are you ☐

    When can we play ☐

    1 mark

3. Add '*f*' or '**ph**' to the words below.
    Use the **pictures** to help you.

    Hassan has a ....**one**.

    I count my ....**ingers**.

    2 marks

---

4. **Rearrange** the letters in the boxes to make two words with the '**ear**' sound. The **first letter** of each word is in **bold**.

| e | **n** | r | a |

| r | e | **c** | e | h |

....

2 marks

5. Put these sentences in the **right order** to tell a story. Write either **1**, **2**, **3** or **4** in the boxes to show the order.

☐ I build a sandcastle.

☐ We walk onto the beach.

☐ We drive to the seaside.

☐ We drive home.

4 marks

Score: ☐

Warm up

1. Add the missing **letters** to each of the words below.
    Use the **pictures** to help you.

b...............   n...............

1 mark

2. **Circle** the words which are **spelt correctly**.

    wood / wud   tuk / took

2 marks

3. **Tick** the words that have a **hard c** sound.

    kids ☐   risky ☐   icy ☐

    face ☐   place ☐   mice ☐

2 marks

4. Put these words in the **right order** to make a sentence. Write either **1**, **2**, **3** or **4** in the boxes to show the order.

I   Simon   with   paint

☐   ☐   ☐   ☐

1 mark

5. **Write** the sentences below using **capital letters**.

my name is noah. i have a
sister called alice.

....

....

....

....

4 marks

Score: ☐

(10)

Warm up

1. **Cross out** the words which are **spelt wrong**.

highest / highist

lowesst / lowest

_____
2 marks

2. **Circle** the correct word to complete each sentence.

My cat likes to **pirr / purr**.

Fold the **papur / paper** in half.

_____
2 marks

3. The words below are **spelt wrong**.
   Rewrite them with the **correct spelling** on the lines.

howse ....

scool ....

_____
2 marks

4. Complete the **singular** words below with '**s**' or '**es**' to make them **plural**.

Singular words tell you that there's <u>only one</u> of something. Plural words tell you that there's <u>more than one</u>.

inch..........   tail..........

2 marks

5. **Read** the sentences. Then **circle** the picture which matches each pair of sentences.

My body is very long.
I don't have any legs.

You find me in the sea.
I have two big claws.

2 marks

Score:

Summer Term: Workout 4

Warm up

1. **Circle** the words which are **spelt correctly**.

   inck / ink   thank / thannk

   2 marks

2. Complete each word with the correct **pair of consonants**. Use the **pictures** to help you.

   ....ain   ....ate

   2 marks

3. Fill in each gap with the **correct letter** from the box. Choose whether or not it should be a **capital letter**. You can only use each letter **once**.

   | e | p | c | i |

   ..... am having a .....**arty**. My friends
   .....**mma** and Oliver are .....**oming**.

   2 marks

4. **Circle** the **correct spelling** of each day of the week.

Thirsday / **Thursday**

Friday / Fryday

5. Look at the **pictures** below. Then read the **sentences**. Write the **correct name** below each sentence.

Sarah   **Nick**   **Abdul**

I like to read and I listen to music.

....

I play sport and I like to bake cookies.

....

Score:

10

1. Add 's' or 'es' to the words in bold
    to complete the sentences.

    She **feed**.......... the hamster.

    The hamster **eat**......... the food.

    _____
    2 marks

2. Split these words into **syllables**.

    party   ....

    tower   ....

    _____
    2 marks

3. Add a **pair of letters** to complete the words below.
    Each word contains the '**or**' sound.
    Use the **pictures** to help you.

    My leg is **s**.........**e**.

    I like tomato **s**.........**ce**.

    _____
    2 marks

4. **Tick** the box where '**and**' should go in this sentence.

My grandad has ☐ a piano ☐
he plays it ☐ every day.

1 mark

5. Add a **letter** or a **pair of letters** to the words in bold to show that there is **more than one** of them. Then **write out** the full sentence on the lines below.

Sona saw some **bird**..........
in the **bush**...........

....

....

....

3 marks

Score: ☐

Warm up

1. Circle the word that is **spelt wrong**.
    Rewrite it with the **correct spelling** on the line.

    match   pach

    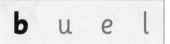

    _____
    2 marks

2. **Rearrange** the letters in the boxes to make two words with
    the 'oo' sound. The **first letter** of each word is in **bold**.

    | **b** | u | e | l |

    | u | e | **t** | b |

    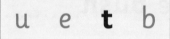

    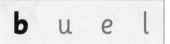

    _____
    2 marks

3. **Circle** a **question mark** or an **exclamation mark**
    to end each sentence.

    What do you want **?** **!**

    How tired I am **?** **!**

    _____
    2 marks

4. Look at the sentence below. **Circle** all the words that should have an 'h' after the 'w'.

I wear my wite winter coat wen it's cold.

2 marks

5. Oscar goes shopping and buys five items.
   Look at the **pictures** below, then **answer** the questions.

shirt

watch

notebook

trousers

bananas

What did Oscar **not** buy?

food ☐   shoes ☐   a book ☐

Which item tells Oscar the time?

....

2 marks

Score: ☐

61

Warm up

1. **Circle** the words which have a **hard c** sound.

    peace   city   keys

        kit   nice

    _____
    1 mark

2. Add a **pair of letters** to complete the words below.
    Each word contains the '**ai**' sound.
    Use the **pictures** to help you.

    I hold the **tr**...........

    She **w**..........**ts** for the bus.

    _____
    2 marks

3. Add the **three** missing **full stops**
    to the sentences below.

    Mason has a parrot Its name is
    Polly It can talk to you

    _____
    3 marks

62

4. The word below is **spelt wrong**. **Rewrite** it with the **correct spelling** on the line. Use the **picture** to help you.

familee

....

1 mark

5. **Join** these sentences together using the word '**and**'. **Write** the new sentence on the lines.

I went to the shop.
Then I walked home.

....

....

....

3 marks

Score:

Warm up

1. **Cross out** the word that is **spelt wrong**.

   give   save   proov

   _____
   1 mark

2. The word below is **spelt wrong**.
   Rewrite it with the **correct spelling** on the line.

   clearrest

   ....

   _____
   1 mark

3. **Circle** the **correct spelling** of the words
   in **bold** to complete the sentences.

   I play for the school **teem / team**.

   He has **three / thrie** teddy bears.   _____
   2 marks

4. Look at the sentences below.
   Circle the **four** words which need a **capital letter**.

   Jo and i went to france.

   We go to london on saturday.

   2 marks

5. Put these sentences in the **right order** to tell a story.
   Write either **1**, **2**, **3** or **4** in the boxes to show the order.

   ☐ I crack the egg.

   ☐ I put the egg on some toast.

   ☐ I eat it all.

   ☐ I fry the egg in a pan.

   4 marks

   Score: ☐

Summer Term: Workout 9

Warm up

1. **Circle** the word that is **spelt correctly**.

    walkker   finder   keepper

2. **Cross out** the words that are **spelt incorrectly**.

    soyl / soil   enjoy / enjoi

3. Look at the **pictures** below. The names of the things in each pair can be **joined together** to make a **new word**. **Write** the new words on the lines.

    ....

    ....

4. **Draw lines** to match each word to its **opposite**.

happy	undress
dress	unpack
pack	unhappy

3 marks

5. **Read** the letter. Then **answer** the questions.

Dear Aunt Lily,

Thank you for my present. I promise to look after it. I will walk it every day and we will play fetch in the garden.

Love from Mo.

Who is Mo writing to?

....

What do you think Mo's present is?

....

2 marks

Score:

Warm up

1. **Circle** the words that are **spelt correctly**.

    marry / marrie   dusti / dusty ____

2. **Complete** the words in **bold** with the correct pair of **double letters** from the box.

ll	ck	ss

    You can only use each pair of letters once.

    I put the key in the **lo**..........

    The dog chases the **ba**..........

    Clean up your **me**.........!

3. Complete the word with the correct **pair of consonants**. Use the **picture** to help you.

    ....im

4. **Rewrite** the word below with the endings '**ed**' and '**ing**'.
   Write the **two** new words on the line.

wash	**+**	ed
		ing

   ....

5. **Read** the story. Then **answer** the questions.

   > Jess the horse lives on a busy farm. She gets scared very
   > easily. She is afraid of the farmer's tractor and the cows.
   > When they come near, she always runs away from them.

   # **Where** does Jess live?

   ....

   # **What two things** is Jess afraid of?

   ....

   ....

   Score:

🕙 10

1. Circle the word which is **spelt wrong**.
    Rewrite it with the **correct spelling** on the line.

    roling   holding

    ....

    2 marks

2. Look at the **pictures** below. The name of each thing
    can be **joined together** to make a **new word**.
    Write the new word on the line.

    = ...

    1 mark

3. **Rearrange** the letters in the boxes to make two words with
    the **short e** sound. The **first letter** of each word is in **bold**.

    | e | d | **h** | a |

    | o | **l** | m | n | e |

    ....

    2 marks

4. Add **full stops** to the sentences below.
   Circle all the words that need a **capital letter**.

   it is raining outside liz
   forgot to wear a coat

   2 marks

5. **Read** the story. Then **answer** the questions.

   > The king was upset. He had lost his crown. He
   > asked the prince to look for it. The prince found the
   > crown under the king's bed. The king felt very silly.

   What had the king lost?

   ....

   Who looked for it?

   ....

   Where did they find it?

   ....

   3 marks

   Score:

Warm up

1. **Circle** the **correct spelling** of the day of the week.

    Wednesday   /   Wensday

    _____
    1 mark

2. Write the **correct spelling** of the word in **bold** on the line.

    Jim saw an **elefant**.

    ....

    _____
    1 mark

3. The words below are **spelt wrong**. **Rewrite** them with the **correct spelling** on the line. Use the **pictures** to help you.

    farey   repear   squair

    ....

    _____
    3 marks

4. Add a **question mark** or an **exclamation mark** to the end of these sentences.

What a pretty shell that is ☐

What colour is the shell ☐

2 marks

5. **Read** the story. Then **answer** the questions.

> Amy the fish was scared of nothing. She wanted to explore the sea, but her mum would not let her. She said it was full of danger. Amy thought this was very unfair.

Which word best describes Amy?

bored ☐   brave ☐   happy ☐

What does Amy want to do?

....

Amy's mum says the sea is:

deep ☐   warm ☐   unsafe ☐

3 marks

Score: ☐

Progress Chart

Fill in the progress chart after you finish each workout.

Put your scores in here to see how you've done.
Each workout is out of 10 marks.

	Autumn Term	Spring Term	Summer Term
Workout 1			
Workout 2			
Workout 3			
Workout 4			
Workout 5			
Workout 6			
Workout 7			
Workout 8			
Workout 9			
Workout 10			
Workout 11			
Workout 12			

Answers

Autumn Term

Workout 1 — pages 2-3

1.   hee   1 mark

2.   be**ll**   1 mark
     cli**ff**   1 mark
     do**ll**   1 mark

3.   James likes jam.   1 mark

4.   rail   1 mark
     tail   1 mark

5.

     | 4 | 1 | 3 | 2 |

     1 mark for each correct answer

Workout 2 — pages 4-5

1.   ra**t**   1 mark
     bi**n**   1 mark
     bo**x**   1 mark

2.   pink   1 mark
     bank   1 mark

3.   leg   1 mark
     beg   1 mark

4.   We went to the park.   1 mark
     Ellie loves her dog.   1 mark

5.   1 mark for copying the sentence correctly

Workout 3 — pages 6-7

1.   gow   1 mark

2.   ki**ss**   1 mark
     dre**ss**   1 mark
     fi**zz**   1 mark

3.   hook   1 mark

4.   (the) cat chases a mouse.   1 mark

5.

     1 mark for each correct answer

Workout 4 — pages 8-9

1.   catch   1 mark

2.   tni   1 mark
     oen   1 mark

3.   ch**air**   p**air**   1 mark for completing both
     words correctly, and 1 mark for matching both
     words to the correct pictures

4.   Bob walks home.   1 mark
     The bird is singing.   1 mark

5.   There is my cat.   1 mark for each space
     correctly added to the sentence

Workout 5 — pages 10-11

1.   wil   1 mark

2.   pack   1 mark
     clock   1 mark

3.   right   1 mark
     kite   1 mark

4.   cows   1 mark
     cards   1 mark

5.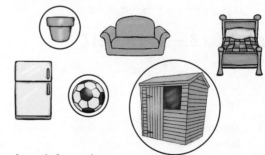

     1 mark for each correct answer

Answers

Workout 6 — pages 12-13

1. I clean the window.   1 mark

2. p**i**g   1 mark
   b**a**t   1 mark
   c**u**p   1 mark

3. The wolf lives in a **cave**.   1 mark

4. saw   1 mark
   corn   1 mark

5. He digs a hole.   1 mark for each space
   correctly added to the sentence

Workout 7 — pages 14-15

1. arr   1 mark

2. park   1 mark
   mark   1 mark

3. apples   apple   church   churches

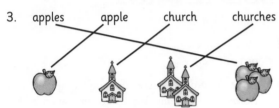

   2 marks for all 4 correct, otherwise
   1 mark for any 2 correct

4. **un**tie   1 mark

5.

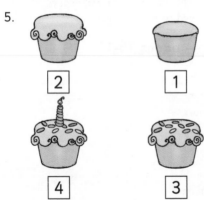

   1 mark for each correct answer

Workout 8 — pages 16-17

1. photo   1 mark

2. jet — V   1 mark
   li**p** — C   1 mark

3. sp**oo**n   1 mark
   b**lew**   1 mark

4. harry   i   1 mark for each correct answer

5. Jane drinks some water.   1 mark for each space
   correctly added to the sentence

Workout 9 — pages 18-19

1. yoo   1 mark

2. kite   keep   1 mark for each correct answer

3. We saw a tree.   1 mark

4. deer   hear   1 mark for each correct answer

5.

   1 mark for each correct answer

Workout 10 — pages 20-21

1. colder   1 mark

2. p**o**t   1 mark
   v**a**n   1 mark
   n**e**t   1 mark

3. coin   1 mark

4.

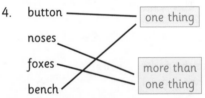

   2 marks for all 4 correct, otherwise
   1 mark for any 2 correct

5. **S**he brushed her teeth.   1 mark for
   correctly using a capital letter, 1 mark for
   correctly using a full stop, and 1 mark
   for correctly rewriting the sentence

Workout 11 — pages 22-23

1. Sunday   1 mark

2. C V C C
2 marks for all 4 correct, otherwise
1 mark for any 2 correct

3. buying   finding   1 mark for each correct answer

4. I st**ir** the mixture.   1 mark
My rabbit has long **fur**.   1 mark
I like your sh**ir**t.   1 mark

5. Abed lost his sock**s**.   1 mark for adding
's' to the end of 'sock', and 1 mark for
correctly copying out the sentence

Workout 12 — pages 24-25

1. h**an**d   1 mark
m**i**lk   1 mark

2. (t r)i p   1 mark
(c l)o s e   1 mark

3. pul   twoday   1 mark for each correct answer

4. I saw a tiger.   1 mark
My aunt lives there.   1 mark

5. 2 marks for copying both sentences correctly,
otherwise 1 mark for copying one sentence
correctly

Spring Term

Workout 1 — pages 26-27

1. luk   intoo   1 mark for each correct answer

2. I like ham and cheese.   1 mark
The dog is black and white.   1 mark

3. whale   1 mark

4. c**o**ne   so**a**p   1 mark for each correct answer

5. Josh   1 mark
Amir   1 mark
Fatima   1 mark

Workout 2 — pages 28-29

1. sp**o**t   1 mark
pl**u**m   1 mark

2.
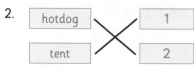

1 mark for each correct answer

3. went   Paul   London   to
[2]   [1]   [4]   [3]
1 mark for all 4 correct

4. My f**eet** are large.   1 mark
We play in the f**ield**.   1 mark
It is nice to m**eet** you.   1 mark

5. The dog chews the bone.   2 marks for all 4 spaces
correctly added, otherwise 1 mark for any 2 spaces
correctly added

Workout 3 — pages 30-31

1. sume   ful   1 mark for each correct answer

2. I am tall **and** he is short.   1 mark
I am quiet **and** she is loud.   1 mark

3. c**ow**   cl**ou**d
1 mark for each correct answer

4. happy   1 mark
funny   1 mark

5. Beth washed the glass**es**.   1 mark for adding 'es'
to the end of 'glass', and 1 mark for rewriting the
sentence correctly

Workout 4 — pages 32-33

1. woz   doun   1 mark both correct

2. packed   1 mark

3. b**ar**k   j**ar**
1 mark for each correct answer

4. two plant**s**   two dress**es**
1 mark for each correct answer

5.

1 mark for each correct answer

Workout 5 — pages 34-35

1. p**ost** f**ish** 1 mark for each correct answer

2. foot**ball** 1 mark
   butterfly 1 mark

3. (f)ro g   (s h)o w   1 mark for both correct

4. How hungry I am!
   1 mark for putting a tick next to this sentence
   What time is it?
   1 mark for putting a cross next to this sentence

5. My mum eats ice cream. She enjoys it.
   1 mark for each correctly placed full stop, and
   1 mark for correctly rewriting the sentences

Workout 6 — pages 36-37

1. s**te**p   g**ri**n   1 mark for both correct

2. The snake hi**ss**ed.   1 mark
   The hi**ll** is over there.   1 mark

3. vet   red   1 mark for each correct answer

4. **e**ngland   **d**aniel   1 mark for each correct answer

5. no   1 mark
   yes   1 mark
   yes   1 mark

Workout 7 — pages 38-39

1. **un**do   **un**roll   1 mark for both correct

2. ask   your   1 mark for each correct answer

3. The si**nk** was full of water.   1 mark
   I thi**nk** it is correct.   1 mark

4. hair   scare   1 mark for each correct answer

5. **W**e go to the zoo. **I**t is lots of fun.
   1 mark for each correct capital letter, and
   1 mark for correctly rewriting the sentences

Workout 8 — pages 40-41

1. r**a**sh   h**i**nt   1 mark for both correct

2. b**oi**l   t**oy**s   1 mark for both correct

3. hatch   itch   1 mark for each correct answer

4. The room is clean **and** tidy.   1 mark
   They like to sing **and** dance.   1 mark
   I hate peas **and** beans.   1 mark

5. I am short and I have big eyes.   1 mark for
   joining the sentences together using 'and', and 2
   marks for correctly rewriting both sentences

Workout 9 — pages 42-43

1. My glo**ve**s are orange.   1 mark

2. have   1 mark for circling 'hav', and
   1 mark for rewriting it correctly

3. I **row** the boat.   1 mark
   The **goat** is friendly.   1 mark
   Leela wants to go **home**.   1 mark

4. two bull**s**   1 mark
   two torch**es**   1 mark

5.

   2 marks for all 4 correct, otherwise
   1 mark for any 2 correct

Workout 10 — pages 44-45

1. **b**all   **b**ath   1 mark for both correct

2.

garden	——	2
radio	——	3

   1 mark for each correct answer

3. Digs   in.   1 mark for each correct answer

4. play   game   1 mark for each correct answer

5. She bakes bread **and** she makes cakes.
   1 mark for joining the sentences correctly using
   'and', 1 mark for removing the capital letter from
   the word 'She', and 1 mark for rewriting both
   sentences correctly

Workout 11 — pages 46-47

1. she   1 mark for circling 'shee', and 1 mark for
   rewriting it correctly

2. jumped   wished   1 mark for each correct answer

3. mouse   1 mark

4. Give me a glue sti**ck**.   1 mark
   She li**ck**s her ice lolly.   1 mark

5. How are you**?**   I am very well**.**
   1 mark for a correctly placed question mark, 1 mark for a correctly placed full stop, and 1 mark for correctly rewriting both sentences

Workout 12 — pages 48-49

1. star   flag   1 mark for both correct

2. monday   1 mark
   hannah   1 mark

3. bike   light   1 mark for each correct answer

4. He throw**s** the ball.   1 mark
   She catch**es** it.   1 mark

5. There is a treasure **chest**.   1 mark
   The diver is holding a **shell**.   1 mark
   There are four **fish**.   1 mark

Summer Term

Workout 1 — pages 50-51

1. just   1 mark

2. How old are you**?**
   When can we play**?**
   1 mark for both correct

3. Hassan has a **ph**one.   1 mark
   I count my **f**ingers.   1 mark

4. near   cheer   1 mark for each correct answer

5. 3 — I build a sandcastle.
   2 — We walk onto the beach.
   1 — We drive to the seaside.
   4 — We drive home.
   1 mark for each correct answer

Workout 2 — pages 52-53

1. belt   nest   1 mark for both correct

2. wood   took   1 mark for each correct answer

3. kids   risky   1 mark for each correct answer

4. I   Simon   with   paint
   [1]   [4]   [3]   [2]

   1 mark for all 4 correct

5. **M**y name is **N**oah. **I** have a sister called **A**lice.
   1 mark for each correct capital letter

Workout 3 — pages 54-55

1. highist   lowesst   1 mark for each correct answer

2. purr   paper   1 mark for each correct answer

3. house   school   1 mark for each correct answer

4. inch**es**   tails   1 mark for each correct answer

5.

   1 mark for each correct answer

Workout 4 — pages 56-57

1. ink   thank   1 mark for each correct answer

2. **t**rain   **pl**ate   1 mark for each correct answer

3. **I** am having a **p**arty. My friends **E**mma and Oliver are **c**oming.
   2 marks for all 4 correct, otherwise 1 mark for any 2 correct

4. Thursday   1 mark
   Friday   1 mark

5. Abdul   1 mark
   Sarah   1 mark

Workout 5 — pages 58-59

1. She feed**s** the hamster.   1 mark
   The hamster eat**s** the food.   1 mark

2. par ty   1 mark
   tow er   1 mark

3. My leg is **s**ore.   1 mark
   I like tomato sa**u**ce.   1 mark

4. My grandad has a piano **and** he plays it every day.   1 mark

5. Sona saw some bird**s** in the bush**es**.
   1 mark for each correct ending, and 1 mark for correctly rewriting the sentence

Answers

Workout 6 — pages 60-61

1. patch   1 mark for circling 'pach', and
   1 mark for rewriting it correctly

2. blue   tube   1 mark for each correct answer

3. What do you want**?**   1 mark
   How tired I am**!**   1 mark

4. I wear my (wite) winter coat (wen) it's cold.
   1 mark for each correct answer

5. shoes   1 mark
   watch   1 mark

Workout 7 — pages 62-63

1. keys   kit   1 mark for both correct

2. I hold the tr**ay**.   1 mark
   She w**ai**ts for the bus.   1 mark

3. Mason has a parrot**.** Its name is Polly**.** It can talk
   to you**.**   1 mark for each correctly placed full stop

4. family   1 mark

5. I went to the shop **and** then I walked home.
   1 mark for joining the sentences correctly
   using 'and', 1 mark for removing the capital
   letter from the word 'Then', and 1 mark
   for rewriting both sentences correctly

Workout 8 — pages 64-65

1. proov   1 mark

2. clearest   1 mark

3. I play for the school **team**.   1 mark
   He has **three** teddy bears.   1 mark

4. Jo and (i) went to (france)   1 mark
   We go to (london) on (saturday)   1 mark

5. 1 — I crack the egg.
   3 — I put the egg on some toast.
   4 — I eat it all.
   2 — I fry the egg in a pan.
   1 mark for each correct answer

Workout 9 — pages 66-67

1. finder   1 mark

2. soyl   enjoi   1 mark for each correct answer

3. cowboy   1 mark
   starfish   1 mark

4.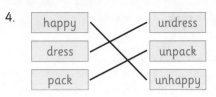

   1 mark for each correct answer

5. Aunt Lily   1 mark
   E.g. a dog   1 mark for any sensible answer

Workout 10 — pages 68-69

1. marry   dusty   1 mark for each correct answer

2. I put the key in the lo**ck**.
   The dog chases the ba**ll**.
   Clean up your me**ss**!   2 marks for all 3 correct,
   otherwise 1 mark for any 2 correct

3. **sw**im   1 mark

4. washed   washing
   1 mark for each correct answer

5. E.g. on a busy farm   1 mark
   the farmer's tractor   1 mark
   the cows   1 mark

Workout 11 — pages 70-71

1. rolling   1 mark for circling 'roling', and
   1 mark for rewriting it correctly

2. sunflower   1 mark

3. head   lemon   1 mark for each correct answer

4. (it) is raining outside**.** (liz) forgot to wear a coat**.**
   1 mark for both correctly placed full stops,
   and 1 mark for circling both correct words

5. his crown   1 mark
   the prince   1 mark
   under the king's bed   1 mark

Workout 12 — pages 72-73

1. Wednesday   1 mark

2. elephant   1 mark

3. fairy   repair   square
   1 mark for each correct answer

4. What a pretty shell that is**!**   1 mark
   What colour is the shell**?**   1 mark

5. brave   1 mark
   explore the sea   1 mark
   unsafe   1 mark

E1XW11